WACKY WORLD of SPORTS

WACKY RACES

Alix Wood

 Gareth Stevens
PUBLISHING

Please visit our website, **www.garethstevens.com**. For a free color catalog of all our high-quality books, call toll free 1-800-542-2595 or fax 1-877-542-2596.

Library of Congress Cataloging-in-Publication Data

Wood, Alix.
Wacky races / by Alix Wood.
p. cm. — (Wacky world of sports)
Includes index.
ISBN 978-1-4824-1222-2 (pbk.)
ISBN 978-1-4824-1242-0 (6-pack)
ISBN 978-1-4824-1498-1 (library binding)
1. Racing — Juvenile literature. 2. Sports — Miscellanea — Juvenile literature. I. Wood, Alix. II. Title.
GV1018.W66 2014
796.7—d23

First Edition

Published in 2015 by
Gareth Stevens Publishing
111 East 14th Street, Suite 349
New York, NY 10003

Produced for Gareth Stevens by Alix Wood Books
Designed by Alix Wood
Picture and content research: Kevin Wood
Editor: Eloise Macgregor

Photo credits:
Cover, 6-7, 12, 28 © Corbis; 1, 4-5, 10-11, 11 inset, 29 © Shutterstock; 8 © Stanislaw Tokarski/Shutterstock; 9 © iStock; 13 © Laszlo Szirtesi/Shutterstock; 14-15 © BluIz60/Shutterstock; 16-17 © Johnjewell/Dreamstime; 17 inset © Gunter Hofer/Dreamstime; 18-19 © Sean Donohue Photo/Shutterstock; 20, 21 © Glynnis Jone/Shutterstock.com; 22 © paintings/Shutterstock; 23 © Brendan Howard/Shutterstock; 24 © Calibas; 25 © Canterbury Oast Trust & Rare Breeds Centre, Kent; 26 © Lestalorm; 27 © Padmayogini/Shutterstock.

Printed in the United States of America

CPSIA compliance information: Batch # CS15GS: For further information contact Gareth Stevens, New York, New York at 1-800-542-2595.

Contents

Wacky sports can be dangerous.
Do not attempt any of the sports
in this book without supervision
from a trained adult expert!

Wacky Races

People around the world love to race, and they love to watch races, too. Some races can be quite crazy! Would you believe there is a boat race in Australia held on a bone–dry river? Even stranger, in Finland, they compete in a wife carrying race! Racing on the back of a bad-tempered water buffalo is pretty weird, too!

Thailand's **annual** Water Buffalo Racing Championships are certainly wacky. Riders balance bareback on buffalo as they thunder down the race track. Most don't manage to stay on. **Spectators** run quite a risk, too. A thin plastic barrier is usually all that separates the track from the seats where the crowd sits watching. The barrier definitely wouldn't stop a charging buffalo!

WACKY SPORTS NEWS

The town of Chonburi, south of Bangkok in Thailand, is host to the National Water Buffalo Racing Festival. To get ready for the race, the buffalo are fed a special diet of eggs and beer. They are trained like rodeo horses before the race. They do not have to work in the fields like the other water buffalo.

Bangkok, Thailand

WACKY FACT
A water tanker is on standby at the Festival. Farmhands follow the buffalo as they are paraded around the arena, throwing buckets of water on them to keep them cool.

Wife Carrying

The Wife Carrying World Championships are held annually in Sonkajärvi, Finland. Men carrying "wives" race through an obstacle course of sand, water, and fences. The prize is the wife's weight in beer! Legend says that long ago in Finland, men stole other men's wives from neighboring villages. To practice for the raids, they would see how fast they could run while carrying a woman. There are prizes for fancy dress and a bonus prize for the husband who completes the course with the heaviest wife!

WACKY FACT

Celebrity and former US NBA basketball star Dennis Rodman competed at Sonkajärvi, although he only ran the last bit of the course. He claimed he wasn't prepared for such a **grueling** contest.

WACKY SPORTS NEWS

Finnish wife-carrying race rules are strict. The first rule is that everyone involved must have fun. You can carry your own wife, your neighbor's wife, or someone found "further afield." The wife must be more than 17 years of age and weigh a minimum of 108 pounds (49 kg), or else she must carry a weighted rucksack to make up the difference! If a contestant drops his wife, he gets a 15-second penalty. Wives are dropped all the time, so they must wear helmets!

Sonkajärvi, Finland

Holds include the piggy-back, fireman's carry, and the Estonian hold. Both these teams are doing versions of the Estonian hold. The man on the right is pushing his wife's legs down to help keep her head out of the water!

Soap Box Derbies

Soap box derbies are races of handmade cars **fueled** by nothing but courage and **gravity**. Soap box derby cars have no engines. Some races supply the cars as kits beforehand for the participants to build themselves. Other races, like the one pictured below, let car builders' imaginations run wild!

WACKY FACT

Soap box racing got its name because the cars were originally made using old wooden soap crates and roller skate wheels.

In some races, finishing first doesn't mean you'll automatically win. Some races are judged on **showmanship** and how creative the soap box design is.

WACKY SPORTS NEWS

There can be scandal even in a wacky sport like soap box racing. In 1973, in Akron, Ohio, a 14-year-old boy was stripped of his title two days after winning the All-American Soap Box Derby! People became suspicious when he had a sudden lead just after each heat began. X-rays of his car found an **electromagnet** in the nose! The electromagnet pulled the car forward when the steel paddle was used to start the race.

Akron, Ohio

Soap box race tracks usually start with a ramp at the top of a hill. The riders want to pick up as much speed as they can at the start to last them to the end of the race. The soap box cars often reach speeds of over 35 miles (56 km) per hour!

The pins are about to be removed and these racers will begin the downhill race in their homemade cars.

pin

9

Crazy Camel Racing

The camels in the picture below don't appear to have anyone riding them. Look closer! There are tiny robots strapped to these camels' backs. Camel racing is a very popular sport in Pakistan, the Middle East, Australia, and Mongolia. Camels can run at about the same speed as a horse. They can run over very long distances.

WACKY FACT

Racing camels used to be ridden by small children, sometimes as young as four years old. Nowadays, in most countries, tiny robots ride the camels instead.

These strange robot jockeys have small hinged arms that control the whip and reins. The robots are **remote controlled** by operators who are driven alongside the race track in SUVs!

The robot jockeys wear clothes and hats, called "silks," in their camel owner's colors.

North Africa

Arabian Peninsula

WACKY SPORTS NEWS

Camel racing is a traditional sport of the Bedouin, who live in the Arabian Peninsula and North Africa. The camels are followed by a pack of cars that race each other to cheer on their favorite. These jockeys are not robots, but young boys around eleven years old. Some of them take a year out of school to train!

The Mascot Grand National

Where can you see a reindeer racing a giraffe? At the annual Mascot Grand National at Kempton Park Racecourse, England! The race has been held since 1999, with up to 100 mascots in full costume running the course. There are a lot of falls, as many mascots have big fluffy feet and can hardly see where they are going! Mascot racing is a very funny sight and raises a lot of money for charity.

Mr. Bumble, Barnet Soccer Club's mascot, is leading the field!

Mr. Bumble won the race in 2010. The race was not held in 2011. The bee retained his crown when the race was run again in 2012.

WACKY FACT

In 2010, around 40 mascots boycotted the race! The mascots were angry that some of the competitors were not full-time mascots, but amateur sportsmen in lightweight costumes.

Over the years, the race has been won by a bulldog, a hornet, a lion, an owl, a gorilla, a squirrel, a monkey, a stag, and a bear! Mascots with oversized feet are given a head start. Some **underhand** tactics can take place. Mascots have been known to stop and block other competitors during the race. Some have even tried to topple their opposition over at the start!

Some mascot costumes are not very easy to run in!

Wacky Bed Racing

Charities often stage crazy races to help raise money. A bed race held in Atlanta, Georgia, raises money for a charity that supplies furniture for free to people who need it.

Atlanta, Georgia

There are five people on each team. Four people push the bed, and one person has to lie on it. Each team is given a bed on wheels and has exactly 20 minutes to decorate it. The race track is a 100-yard (91.4 m) stretch of street in the center of Atlanta. There are prizes for the best costume, best bed design, and the fastest finish time.

WACKY FACT

In Knaresborough, UK, a bed race has been held each year since 1966. Teams decorate their beds according to a theme. The passengers must wear a helmet and life jacket. After the teams run up the steep hill to the castle, they run back down again and must cross a wide river at the bottom. Many beds sink!

A team hurtles around a corner during the Atlanta bed race.

WACKY SPORTS NEWS

Friedrichroda, Germany, stages a bed race that involves challenges along the route. Two team members have to cut through a log using a two-man saw. The passenger on the bed has to carefully guide a hoop around a wire circuit without setting off a buzzer. The team also has to pump water through a fire hose to blast six bottles off a stand. The team navigates a slalom of cones and a water-filled **gully** and tunnel, too!

Friedrichroda, Germany

Henley-on-Todd Boat Race

The weather can get pretty dry in central Australia. The people of Alice Springs wanted to hold a boat race. The fact that Alice Springs is 930 miles (1,500 km) from the nearest large body of water was never seen as a problem! The Henley-on-Todd Regatta is a "boat" race held annually in the typically dry, sandy bed of the Todd River in Alice Springs, Australia. Every year in the spring, around September, the town holds a mock **regatta**. It is the only dry river regatta in the world. "Boats" are made from metal frames and teams of "rowers" run their boats in races through the hot sand.

WACKY SPORTS NEWS

In 1993, the event had to be cancelled after heavy rains meant water actually appeared in the river!

Alice Springs, Australia

WACKY FACT

The Todd River regatta began as a joke, poking fun at the formal atmosphere of the British river race, the Henley-on-Thames Royal Regatta, shown below.

FOUR WHEEL DRIVE CLUB

Outhouse Racing

At the winter carnival in Lake George, New York, teams compete against each other in a fun race to see who has the fastest outhouse!

WACKY FACT

Teams are made up of two pushers, two pullers, and one "sitter." Each racing outhouse must contain a toilet seat and a toilet paper dispenser. The outhouse must be mounted on skis.

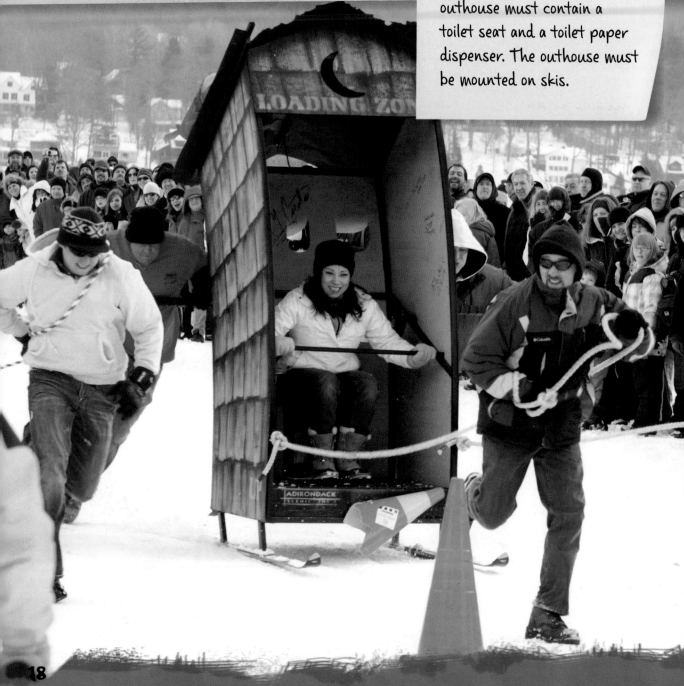

WACKY SPORTS NEWS

There's no snow in Des Moines, Iowa, in August, so their outhouses have to have wheels instead of skis. They race along an obstacle course, where teams have to dig through mucky pig feed and sit on a toilet seat with chocolate sauce on it. The winners take home a gold-painted toilet seat as a trophy.

Des Moines, Iowa

Through Mud and Fire

Some people think simply running a race is too dull. Instead, why not run through burning hay bales while choking on the smoke? Or maybe crawl through a field of mud with a shocking electric current inches above your head? This is the tough world of the crazy mud runners!

One extreme race is called the "Tough Mudder." It is a long obstacle course designed by UK Special Forces to test strength, stamina, mental grit, and teamwork. The races are held all around the world.

A team crawls through a mud pit surrounded by electrified wires during the grueling Tough Mudder course.

Participants run among pits of blazing firewood, jump a fire pit, and plunge into a pit of ice cold water.

WACKY SPORTS NEWS

These extreme courses have been designed to be very tough, but they're still safe. Race organizers have experts on hand to check the safety of every obstacle and medical teams on standby if anything goes wrong. Do not attempt any of these challenges yourself.

Racing Santas

Many countries around the world hold Santa races, especially around Christmastime. Entrants must dress as Santa Claus. Sometimes elves and reindeer costumes are allowed, too. The races are a fun way to raise money for charity.

Derry, Northern Ireland

Porto, Portugal

WACKY SPORTS NEWS

Sometimes a Santa race can be a race to get in the world record books. 12,965 people dressed as Santa gathered in Derry City, Northern Ireland, in 2007. In 2008, over 14,200 people dressed as Santa were estimated to have attended a gathering in Porto, Portugal! Derry still holds the official record, though.

In Brisbane, Australia, the weather around Christmastime is warm. Their Santa race costume has shorts instead of pants to help the runners keep cool in the hot temperatures. Even so, taking some water along is a good idea!

At some Santa races, prizes are given for the best decorated baby stroller, or the best dog costume.

Hundreds of Santas take part in a race in Princes Street Gardens, Edinburgh, Scotland.

WACKY FACT

The Great Scottish Santa Race in Edinburgh provides a Santa outfit when you register. The organizers recommend you take your own belt, though, as the pants have been known to fall down and become a tripping hazard!

Pig Racing

Pigs may not seem like the ideal racing animal at first. They are known for being pretty lazy and greedy. Did you know that pigs are actually considered the fourth most intelligent animal on the planet? Young pigs are natural comedians, too, as they race around the track snorting and squealing with their little tails twirling.

Pigs race flat races, or they can race over hurdles, like in the picture below. Some pigs even do a triathlon by jumping into a pool at the end! The water helps to cool them down.

As pigs are **prey** animals, they don't naturally run in a straight line. They swerve and dodge so their predators can't catch them.

Pigs can run about 7 to 11 miles (11 to 17.5 km) per hour.

WACKY FACT

People sometimes place bets on which pig they think will win. The pigs are racing for their own prize, which is often their favorite cookie!

Pig farmers use boards to herd their pigs around the farm. At some pig races, members of the audience volunteer to try their hand at pig herding. It is not as easy as it looks! The pigs often get distracted and sometimes stop in the middle of the track for no apparent reason.

Looks like the red team is going to win this pig race.

Pancake Races

Olney, in England, holds a famous pancake race. Only women who live in the town can take part. The race dates back to 1445. A woman was cooking pancakes and heard the church bell. She was so flustered at being late for church that she ran there in her apron still holding her frying pan!

This competition's rules are strict. Contestants have to toss their pancake at both the start and the finish of the race. They must wear an apron and a headscarf. The traditional prize is a kiss from the **verger**! Since 1950, Olney has competed in an "International Pancake Race" with the town of Liberal, Kansas, for the fastest time in either town.

WACKY FACT

The score for the International Pancake Race stands at 26 wins for Olney and 36 wins for Liberal, with 1 "no contest." In 1980, the score didn't count because a news van blocked the finish line in Olney!

The Olney pancake race.

Every Shrove Tuesday in London, England, members of Parliament put aside running the country to take part in an annual charity pancake race outside the Houses of Parliament. The crowd is mainly full of tourists wondering what on earth is going on. The three teams are from the House of Lords, the House of Commons, and the press.

Pancake races are usually run on Shrove Tuesday, the day before Lent in the Christian calendar. Lent was a time of **fasting**, so people would use up their milk by making pancakes!

Outside the Houses of Parliament in London, UK, Lord Kennedy races for the House of Lords team in the annual Parliamentary Pancake Race.

Garbage Can Racing

The Garbage Can World Championship takes place in Hermeskeil, Germany. The main street is closed off to traffic. Contestants start the race by hurtling down a wooden ramp and then leaning into a sharp corner onto the street. Riding a garbage can is all about technique. The only thing you want touching the road are the two wheels. The riders need to lean their weight back to lift the front end, but keep their legs and feet clear of the road. They want as little contact with the road as possible.

WACKY SPORTS NEWS

The Hermeskeil Garbage Can World Championship organizers apparently got the idea for riding the trash cans when they saw someone lay on a garbage can at a music festival at the German Formula I race track, the Nürburgring.

Hermeskeil, Germany

At the annual Thoona wheelie bin race in Australia, kids and their families work together to create the fastest wheelie bin in the district. The modified garbage cans can have four wheels, but two of them must be the original can's wheels.

WACKY FACT

Competitors must use at least two-thirds of the garbage can in the construction of their racer. They are not allowed any animal, mechanical, or motorized assistance in the race.

A typical wheelie bin racer ready for the Thoona wheelie bin race in Australia.

Glossary

annual
Occurring or performed once a year.

electromagnet
Magnetism developed by a current of electricity.

fasting
To go without eating.

fueled
Powered.

gravity
The force that anchors you to the ground and stops you from floating.

grueling
Requiring extreme effort.

gully
A trench worn in the earth by running water after rains.

prey
An animal hunted or killed by another animal for food.

regatta
A boat race or a series of boat races.

remote controlled
Controlled from a distance by a device.

showmanship
The way you present yourself during a performance or competition.

spectators
People who look on (as at a sports event).

underhand
Done in secret or so as to deceive.

verger
A minor church official.

For More Information

Books

Kelley, K. C. *Weird Races* (Weird Sports). North Mankato, MN: Child's World, 2011.

Neelman, Sol. *Weird Sports*. Heidelberg, Germany: Kehrer Verlag, 2011.

Rooney, Anne. *Wacky Sports*. London, UK: Franklin Watts, 2013.

Websites

Super Healthy Kids
www.superhealthykids.com/blog-posts/10-fun-and-crazy-races-for-kids.php
Lists wacky races that kids can enter, including dressing up as a zombie or glowing in the dark.

Wacky Races Around The World
www.mydestination.com/blog/wacky-races-around-the-world/
A selection of wacky animal races from across the globe.

Index